한글마스터
HANGEUL MASTER

What is Talk To Me In Korean?

Talk To Me In Korean has provided FREE Korean language learning content to people around the globe since 2009. With over 800 lessons published on the official website at TalkToMeInKorean.com, it has become the largest community in the world for Korean learners.

As a community that motivates and nurtures learners to develop their language skills in a variety of fun and innovative ways, Talk To Me In Korean has drawn over 1.9 million people to the website to download over 50 million lessons.

Stop on by *http://www.talktomeinkorean.com* to check it out if you haven't visited before. You'll be glad you did.

한글마스터

written and designed by Talk To Me In Korean

Contents

Chapter I.

THE HISTORY OF 한글
(Hangeul)

Korean is a language spoken by over 74 million people on the Korean peninsula (as of 2012) and millions more throughout the world. Due to the rising popularity of Korean culture, there is an increasing number of people learning Korean as a new language. Korean is written using a featural alphabet called Hangeul (한글), which translates to "great script" in English. Hangeul is considered to be one of the most scientific and efficient writing systems in the world and has been touted as such by language experts around the world.

The History of Hangeul

Before 1446

Before Hangeul was invented, Korean was written using Chinese characters, called Hanja (한자) in Korean, and could only be learned by the elite classes and those who could afford an education. Writing Korean with Chinese characters meant memorizing thousands upon thousands of characters and trying to put them together to apply to Korean. The sounds and grammatical structure of Korean are very different from Chinese; therefore, to write a message using only Hanja was very inefficient.

1446

During the Joseon Dynasty (1392-1910), the fourth king, Sejong the Great (reign: 1418-1450), made it known that he truly despised using Hanja to write Korean. He wanted all his people to be able to read and write, not just those in higher social classes. King Sejong was determined to come up with a new writing system that was easy enough for the common man to learn and could accurately depict the sounds of human speech. He and a committee of scholars set out to do just that, and the result was a 28 letter alphabet now known as Hangeul. The new writing system was officially announced on October 9, 1446 (Gregorian calendar) in a document called 훈민정음 (Hun Min Jeong Eum), which means "The Proper Sounds for the Education of the People". October 9th is now an official national holiday in Korea and is known as 한글날, or "Hangeul Day".

After Hangeul was officially and publicly announced by King Sejong the Great, it was met with some resistance and was not immediately made the official writing system. There were many scholars who opposed the new writing system because they feared it would sour relations with China and that it contradicted certain Neo-Confucian principles. This gave Hangeul a bad reputation and is one of the reasons why the new writing system was not generally accepted at first.

1894

Over time, Hangeul became widely used across the Korean peninsula, but it was still not being used by the majority of people due to lack of public education. In spite of this, the first private newspaper which was written in only Hangeul and English was printed in 1886. Other media sources soon followed, and although a few Hanja characters were still used, there were not as many as before. Nearly a decade later in 1894, it was proclaimed that Hangeul was to be used for official documents and using Hanja was to be a secondary means of explanation. With these big steps toward making Hangeul more popular in Korea, King Sejong's dream of everyone being able to read and write seemed to be on a successful journey.

1910-1945

During the Japanese colonization period of Korea, which lasted from 1910 until 1945, Japanese was made the official language. In order to maintain Korean pride and a cultural identity amidst assimilation into Japan, in the early 1910s, Hangeul was given the name "Hangeul" by Korean language scholars and was published in a Korean magazine called Dongnip Sinmun (독립신문). Additionally, throughout the colonization, Koreans fought to keep the language alive through Korean-language radio programs and teaching Hangeul and spoken Korean at home. Unfortunately, the use of Hangeul and spoken Korean in public and in schools was completely banned in 1938, and soon after, all Korean-language publications were banned in 1941.

1945 ~

After Korea was liberated from Japan in 1945, Korea's desire for independence and a cultural identity was stronger than ever. At that time, many intellectuals and scholars pushed the idea of strictly using 순한글 (sun Hangeul), or "pure Korean", in all texts to help establish identity and independence. In 1988, a brand new newspaper company, called Hangyeore Newspaper (한겨레신문), published its first issue using only Hangeul. Slowly but surely, other newspaper companies followed in Hangyeore's footsteps. You can now find nearly every type of printed publication in Korea from magazines to books, newspapers to comics, using Hangeul.

Despite the hardships of acceptance and surviving through the Japanese colonization, Hangeul has stood strong and prevailed, just like the Korean spirit. This easy-to-learn and practical writing system, which Sejong the Great developed so that his people could read and express themselves in writing, is enjoying widespread use across Korea and throughout the world. Hangeul is considered to be one of the greatest intellectual achievements of all time, and you are about to enter into that world. Can you handle it? Are you ready to become a Hangeul Master?

Let's get started!

Chapter II.

INTRODUCTION TO 한글
(Hangeul)

The Korean alphabet is called **한글** (Hangeul), and there are 24 basic letters and digraphs in **한글**.

*digraph: pair of characters used to make one sound (phoneme)

Of the letters, fourteen are consonants (**자음**), and five of them are doubled to form the five tense consonants (**쌍자음**).

Consonants

Basic	ㄱ	ㄴ	ㄷ	ㄹ	ㅁ	ㅂ	ㅅ	ㅇ	ㅈ	ㅊ	ㅋ	ㅌ	ㅍ	ㅎ
	g/k	n	d/t	r/l	m	b/p	s	ng	j	ch	k	t	p	h
	g/k	n	d/t	r/l	m	b/p	s/ɕ	ŋ	dʑ/tɕ	tɕʰ	k/kʰ	t/tʰ	p/pʰ	h

Tense	ㄲ		ㄸ			ㅃ	ㅆ		ㅉ					
	kk		tt			pp	ss		jj					
	k'		t'			p'	s'		c'					

When it comes to vowels (**모음**), there are 10 basic letters. 11 additional letters can be created by combining certain basic letters to make a total of 21 vowels. Of the vowels, eight are single pure vowels, also known as monophthongs (**단모음**), and 13 are diphthongs (**이중모음**), or two vowel sounds joined into one syllable which creates one sound.

*When saying a monophthong, you are producing one pure vowel with no tongue movement.

*When saying a diphthong, you are producing one sound by saying two vowels. Therefore, your tongue and mouth move quickly from one letter to another (glide or slide) to create a single sound.

Vowels

Monophthongs										
ㅏ	ㅓ	ㅗ	ㅜ	ㅡ	ㅣ	ㅐ	ㅔ			
a	eo	o	u	eu	i	ae	e			
a/aː	ʌ/əː	o/oː	u/uː	ɨ/ɰː	i/iː	ɛ/ɛː	e/eː			

Diphthongs										
ㅑ	ㅕ	ㅛ	ㅠ			ㅒ	ㅖ			
ya	yeo	yo	yu			yae	ye			
ja	jʌ	jo	ju			jɛ	je			
ㅘ	ㅝ					ㅙ	ㅞ			
wa	wo					wae	we			
wa	wʌ/wəː					wɛ	we			
								ㅚ	ㅟ	ㅢ
								oe	wi	ui
								we	wi	ɨi

* ㅚ and ㅟ were pronounced as single pure vowels (monophthongs) in the past; however, presently, these vowels are produced as two vowels gradually gliding into one another to create one sound (diphthong).

Writing 한글 letters

한글 is written top to bottom, left to right. For example:

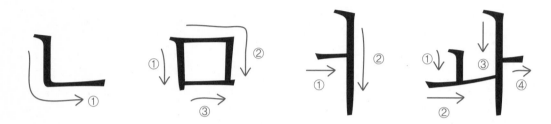

By making sure you follow the stroke order rules, you will find that writing Korean is quite easy and other people will be able to better read your handwriting.

Syllable Blocks

Each Korean syllable is written in a way that forms a block-like shape, with each letter inside the block forming a sound/syllable.

ㅊ + ㅣ + ㄴ (ch+i+n) = chin

ㄱ + ㅜ (g+u) = gu

친 (chin) + 구 (gu) = 친구 (chingu) = "friend"

In each syllable block, there is a:

1. * *Beginning consonant*

2. * *Middle vowel*

3. *Optional final consonant*

* *Required in a syllable block. A block MUST contain a minimum of two letters: 1 consonant and 1 vowel.*

Two of the most common ways to write consonant and vowel combinations in Korean are horizontally and vertically (the boxes drawn here are for illustrative purpose only).

By adding a final consonant (**받침**), the blocks are modified:

There are also syllables which have two final consonants, such as:

C V
C C   ➤   넓, 없, 닭, 앉

In all the syllable blocks, the letters are either compressed or stretched to keep the size relatively the same as the other letters.

Vowels

Since the "minimum two letter" rule exists and one letter has to be a consonant and the other has to be a vowel, what can you do when a vowel needs to be written in its own syllable block? Add the consonant ㅇ [ng] in front of or on top of the vowel. When reading a vowel, such as 아, the ㅇ makes no sound and you just pronounce the ㅏ [a].

*Vowels absolutely, cannot, under any circumstances be written by themselves!!

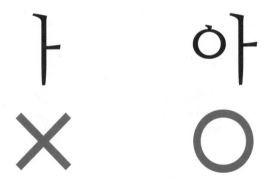

Okay! Now that you are equipped with a very basic knowledge of 한글,
it's time to study the Korean alphabet in more detail so you can truly become a 한글 마스터!
Let's get to it!

Time-Out #1
When Do Koreans Learn Hangeul?

How and when Korean children learn Hangeul can vary depending on the household and the preference of the parents, but on average, most children begin learning between the ages of 3 and 5. In the past, many children began to learn Hangeul right before starting elementary school around the age of 5, but now that pre-elementary school programs are becoming more commonplace in Korea, some children start learning to read and write as early as age 2! There are also many instances of children learning Hangeul at home with instruction from parents or even on their own.

Methods used to teach Hangeul are similar to those used in teaching the English alphabet: letter flashcards, storybooks, writing practice books, etc. Hangeul tends to be more true to the actual sound of a letter, making spelling much less complicated than in English. This means there is less emphasis on spelling drills and dictation exercises, but more emphasis on phonics and correct pronunciation.

LEARN HANGEUL

Unit I. Single Vowels (단모음)

Hangeul	IPA	Sounds like	Hint
ㅏ	[a] [aː]	"a" as in "father"	A

Syllable block	Stroke order	Practice here
C V	↓ㅏ② ①→	아 아 아 아

Hangeul	IPA	Sounds like	Hint
ㅓ	[ʌ] [əː]	"u" as in "bus" or "gut"	ㅓ

Syllable block	Stroke order	Practice here
C V	→ㅓ② ①	어 어 어 어

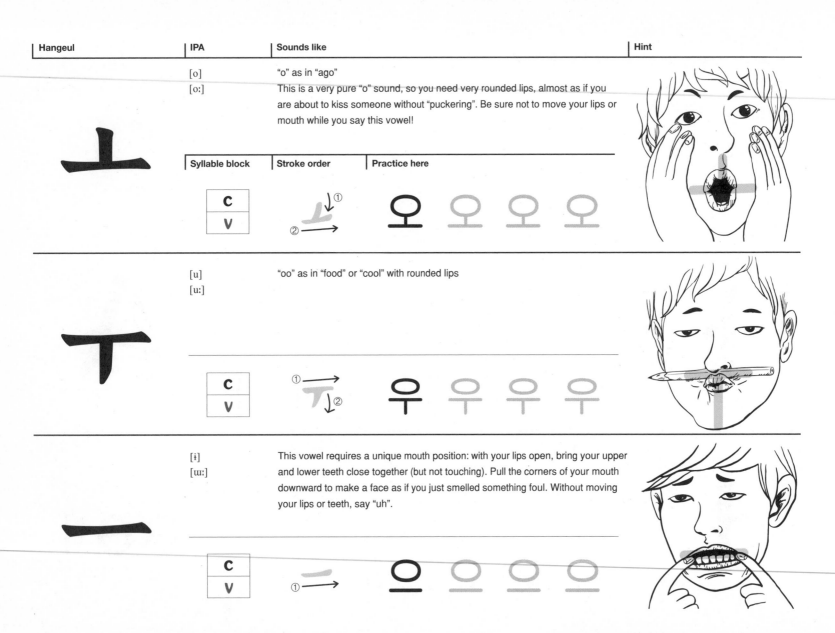

Hangeul	IPA	Sounds like			Hint
ㅗ	[o] [oː]	"o" as in "ago" This is a very pure "o" sound, so you need very rounded lips, almost as if you are about to kiss someone without "puckering". Be sure not to move your lips or mouth while you say this vowel!			
		Syllable block	**Stroke order**	**Practice here**	
		C V	① ② →	오 오 오 오	
ㅜ	[u] [uː]	"oo" as in "food" or "cool" with rounded lips			
		C V	① → ↓②	우 우 우 우	
ㅡ	[ɨ] [ɯː]	This vowel requires a unique mouth position: with your lips open, bring your upper and lower teeth close together (but not touching). Pull the corners of your mouth downward to make a face as if you just smelled something foul. Without moving your lips or teeth, say "uh".			
		C V	① →	으 으 으 으	

Hangeul	IPA	Sounds like		Hint

ㅣ

[i]
[i:]

"ee" as in "feet" or "ea" in "peach"

Syllable block	Stroke order	Practice here
C | V	① ↓	이 이 이 이

I i

ㅐ

[ɛ]
[ɛ:]

"a" as in "sad" or "pan"

A A H

Syllable block	Stroke order	Practice here
C | V	② → ① ↓ ③ ↓	애 애 애 애

ㅔ

[e]
[e:]

"e" as in "bed" or "pet"

* ㅐ and ㅔ are different sounds in theory, but many people pronounce them identically and cannot differentiate the two when listening or speaking.

Syllable block	Stroke order	Practice here
C | V	① → ③ ↓ ② ↓	에 에 에 에

 **Quick Quiz**

Check to see how much you remember!

1. What does ㅏ sound like?

   (1) "a" as in "father"

   (2) "e" as in "bed"

   (3) "o" as in "soda"

   (4) "a" as in "face"

2. Which two vowels sound almost the same?

   (1) 아 and 어

   (2) 오 and 우

   (3) 으 and 이

   (4) 애 and 에

3. How does ㅣ sound?

   (1) "i" as in "side"

   (2) "ee" as in "feet"

   (3) "ea" as in "weather"

   (4) "e" as in "pet"

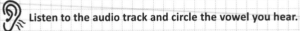 **Listen to the audio track and circle the vowel you hear.**

🎤 **Q1** ⋮ 4. (1) 이 (2) 우 (3) 아 (4) 애

🎤 **Q2** ⋮ 5. (1) 어 (2) 오 (3) 에 (4) 으

🎤 **Q3** ⋮ 6. (1) 아이 (2) 오우 (3) 으애 (4) 어에

🎤 **Q4** ⋮ 7. (1) 우에 (2) 애이 (3) 이오 (4) 아어

You can download the mp3 audio files at www.talktomeinkorean.com/audio.

Answers are on p. 154.

Track 2

Hangeul	IPA	Sounds like	Hint
ㄱ	[g]	"g" as in "go" or "gap", NOT in "genuine" or "giraffe"	

Syllable block	Stroke order	Practice here
C V / C V	ㄱ①	가 가 고 고

| | [n] | "n" as in "no" or "new" with the tongue touching the back of the upper teeth | |

Syllable block	Stroke order	Practice here
C V / C V	ㄴ①	나 나 노 노

Hangeul	IPA	Sounds like	Hint

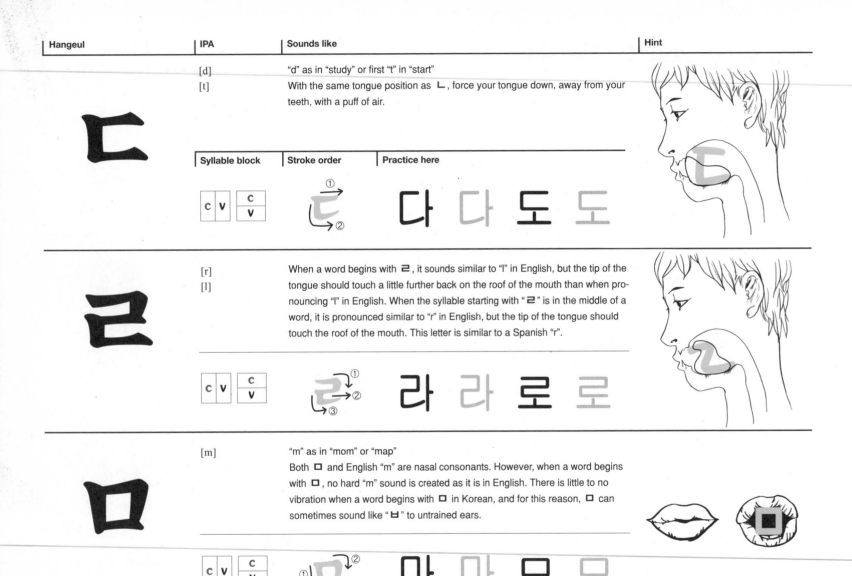

[d]   "d" as in "study" or first "t" in "start"

[t]   With the same tongue position as ㄴ, force your tongue down, away from your teeth, with a puff of air.

Syllable block	Stroke order	Practice here

다 다 도 도

[r]
[l]

When a word begins with ㄹ, it sounds similar to "l" in English, but the tip of the tongue should touch a little further back on the roof of the mouth than when pronouncing "l" in English. When the syllable starting with "ㄹ" is in the middle of a word, it is pronounced similar to "r" in English, but the tip of the tongue should touch the roof of the mouth. This letter is similar to a Spanish "r".

라 라 로 로

[m]   "m" as in "mom" or "map"

Both ㅁ and English "m" are nasal consonants. However, when a word begins with ㅁ, no hard "m" sound is created as it is in English. There is little to no vibration when a word begins with ㅁ in Korean, and for this reason, ㅁ can sometimes sound like "ㅂ" to untrained ears.

아 아 모 모

Hangeul	IPA	Sounds like	Hint

[b]
[p]

"b" as in "busy" or "baby" without vocalization.

ㅂ is pronounced with the same mouth shape as ㅁ, and the added short lines on top represent a puff of air used to separate the lips.

ㅂ

Syllable block	Stroke order	Practice here

C V / C V

바 바 보 보

---

[s]
[ɕ]

"s" as in "slow" or "sh" in "sheep".

Depending on the following vowel, ㅅ sometimes sounds like "s" or "sh" in English. However, it is generally said with less airflow than the English "s".

ㅅ

C V / C V

사 사 소 소

[ŋ]

This consonant has two functions: 1) it does not make any sound when in front of a vowel. The only letter which is pronounced is the following vowel; 2) when ㅇ follows a vowel, it makes a sound like the "ng" in "song" or "ring".

ㅇ

C V / C V

아 아 오 오

Hangeul	IPA	Sounds like	Hint
	[dʑ]	"j" as in "Jill"	
	[tɕ]		

ᄌ

Syllable block	Stroke order	Practice here
C V / C V		자 자 조 조

 *Quick Quiz*

Check to see how much you remember!

 Listen to the audio track and circle the syllable you hear.

1. What does ㄱ sound like?

    (1) "c" as in "cite"

    (2) "c" as in "cat"

    (3) "g" as in "gap"

    (4) "g" as in "giraffe"

Q5   4. (1) 사   (2) 자   (3) 다   (4) 바

Q6   5. (1) 로   (2) 모   (3) 노   (4) 오

Q7   6. (1) 나라   (2) 나마   (3) 라나   (4) 라마

2. Which consonant does not make a sound when written before a vowel?

    (1) ㅈ

    (2) ㅇ

    (3) ㅁ

    (4) ㄷ

Q8   7. (1) 고보   (2) 고모   (3) 도보   (4) 도모

3. How are ㅈ and ㅜ supposed to be written to create a syllable?

    (1) ㅈㅜ

    (2) ㅜㅈ

    (3) ㅈ
       ㅜ

    (4) ㅜ
       ㅈ

Answers are on p. 154.

Track 3

Hangeul	IPA	Sounds like		Hint
	[tɕʰ]	"ch" as in "chain" or "cheat" ㅊ is pronounced with the same tongue position as ㅈ, and the additional line on the top represents a faster and increased airflow.		

ㅊ

	Syllable block	Stroke order	Practice here
	C V / C V	① ② ③	차 차 초 초

Hangeul	IPA	Sounds like		Hint
	[k] [kʰ]	"k" as in "Korea" or "c" in "career" ㅋ is pronounced with the same tongue position as ㄱ, and the additional line represents a faster and increased airflow.		

ㅋ

	Syllable block	Stroke order	Practice here
	C V / C V	① ②	카 카 코 코

Hangeul	IPA	Sounds like	Hint

[t]
[tʰ]

"t" as in "tape" or "teeth"

ㅌ is pronounced with the same tongue position as ㄴ and ㄷ, and the additional line represents a faster and increased airflow.

ㅌ

ㄷ ㅌ

Syllable block	Stroke order	Practice here
C V / C V	① → ② → ③ →	타 타 토 토

[p]
[pʰ]

"p" as in "power" or "permanent"

ㅍ is pronounced with the same mouth shape as ㅁ and ㅂ, but the additional lines represent a faster and increased airflow.

ㅍ

ㅁ

Syllable block	Stroke order	Practice here
C V / C V	① → ② ↓ ③ ↓ ④ →	파 파 포 포

[h]

"h" as in "harmony" or "hat"

ㅎ

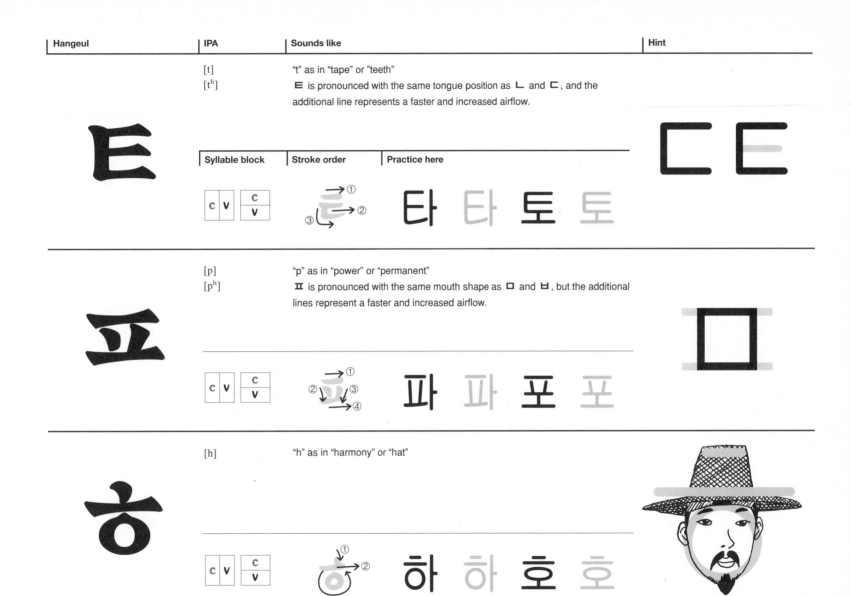

Syllable block	Stroke order	Practice here
C V / C V	① → ② ③	하 하 호 호

 **Quick Quiz**

Check to see how much you remember!

1. What does ㅎ sound like?

(1) "t" as in "tape" or "teeth"

(2) "p" as in "power" or "permanent"

(3) "ch" as in "chain" or "cheat"

(4) "h" as in "harmony" or "happy"

2. Which of the following does not sound like ㅋ?

(1) "c" as in "cat"

(2) "k" as in "kiss"

(3) "c" as in "ceiling"

(4) "k" as in "kitchen"

3. How are ㅌ and ㅓ supposed to be written to create a syllable?

(1) ㅌㅓ

(2) ㅓㅌ

(3) ㅌ
　　ㅓ

(4) ㅓ
　　ㅌ

 Listen to the audio track and circle the syllable you hear.

🎤 **Q9** 　4. (1) 차　(2) 카　(3) 타　(4) 파

🎤 **Q10** 　5. (1) 포　(2) 코　(3) 초　(4) 토

🎤 **Q11** 　6. (1) 초코　(2) 토코　(3) 포호　(4) 호초

🎤 **Q12** 　7. (1) 카초　(2) 코차　(3) 타코　(4) 토카

Answers are on p. 154.

Drills and Exercises (Unit I ~ Unit III)

Fill in the chart

Answers are on p. 154.

	ㄱ	ㄴ	ㄷ	ㄹ	ㅁ	ㅂ	ㅅ	ㅇ	ㅈ	ㅊ	ㅋ	ㅌ	ㅍ	ㅎ	
가															ㅏ
거															ㅓ
															ㅗ
															ㅜ
															ㅡ
															ㅣ
															ㅐ
															ㅔ

Listen to the audio track and complete the syllable. 🎤 **Q13**

| ㅏ | ㅐ | ㅗ | ㅡ | ㅁ | ㅂ | ㅎ | ㅅ |

💭❓
Answers are on p. 154.

Practice reading and writing Korean words using what you have learned so far. 🎤 Track 4

개

바지

코

모자

나무

아기

다리

치마

고래 ___ ___ ___

나비 ___ ___

The following Korean words are all loanwords. Read each loanword aloud and mark the equivalent English word.

라디오   (1) radiator   (2) radio   (3) rabbit   (4) lady

피자   (1) pizza   (2) Fiji   (3) peace   (4) pyjamas/pajamas

버스   (1) but   (2) burst   (3) both   (4) bus

커피   (1) cuppa   (2) coffee   (3) copy   (4) cafe

테이프   (1) taffy   (2) tofu   (3) tape   (4) tap

Answers are on p. 154.

Track 5

Hangeul	IPA	Sounds like	Hint
	[ja]	"ya" as in "yard" or "yarn"	

ㅑ

Syllable block	Stroke order	Practice here
C V		야 야 야 야

ㅣ + ㅏ = ㅑ

| | [jʌ] | "yu" as in "yummy" or "yucky" | |

ㅕ

Syllable block	Stroke order	Practice here
C V		여 여 여 여 여

ㅣ + ㅓ = ㅕ

Hangeul	IPA	Sounds like	Hint
	[jo]	"yo" as in "yogurt" or "yoga"	

Syllable block	Stroke order	Practice here

C
V

| | [ju] | "u" as in "USA" or "Utah" | |

C
V

| | [jɛ] | "ye" as in "yes" or "yet" | |

C	V

Hangeul	IPA	Sounds like		Hint
	[je]	"ye" as in "yes" or "yet"		

Syllable block	Stroke order	Practice here
C V	① → ④ ② → ③	예 예 예 예

$| + || = ||$

 **Quick Quiz**

How much do you remember? Find out with this quiz!

1. What does ㅑ sound like?

    (1) "ye" as in "yes"

    (2) "yu" as in "yummy"

    (3) "yo" as in "yogurt"

    (4) "ya" as in "yard"

2. Which two vowels sound almost the same?

    (1) ㅑ and ㅐ

    (2) ㅓ and ㅖ

    (3) ㅑ and ㅕ

    (4) ㅐ and ㅖ

3. How are ㅐ and ㅈ supposed to be written to create a syllable?

    (1) ㅐㅈ

    (2) ㅈㅐ

    (3) ㅈ
       ㅐ

    (4) ㅐ
       ㅈ

 Listen to the audio track and circle the syllable you hear.

🎤 **Q14** : 4. (1) 갸 (2) 겨 (3) 교 (4) 규

🎤 **Q15** : 5. (1) 쿄 (2) 챠 (3) 폐 (4) 텨

🎤 **Q16** : 6. (1) 유야 (2) 유여 (3) 유예 (4) 유요

🎤 **Q17** : 7. (1) 나뮤 (2) 녀뮤 (3) 냐묘 (4) 녀묘

Answers are on p. 155.

Track 6

Hangeul	IPA	Sounds like
	[wa]	"wa" as in "swan" or "swat"

Syllable block	Stroke order	Practice here
		와 와 와 와 와 와

	[wʌ] [wə:]	"wo" as in "wonderful" or "work"

Syllable block	Stroke order	Practice here
		워 워 워 워 워 워

Hangeul		IPA	Sounds like
		[wɛ]	"we" as in "western" or "wet"

Syllable block	Stroke order	Practice here
		왜 왜 왜 왜 왜 왜

		[we]	"we" as in "western" or "wet"

Syllable block	Stroke order	Practice here
		웨 웨 웨 웨 웨 웨

		[we]	"we" as in "western" or "wet"

The combination of ㅗ and ㅣ looks like it should be pronounced as "oy", but is actually pronounced the same as ㅙ or ㅞ.

Syllable block	Stroke order	Practice here
		외 외 외 외 외 외

Hangeul	IPA	Sounds like
	[wi]	"we" as in "we" or "weekend"

ㅟ

Syllable block	Stroke order	Practice here
C / V / V	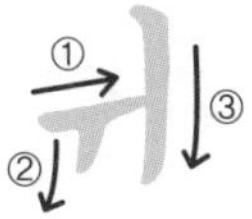 ①→ ㅟ ③↓ ②↙	위 위 위 위 위 위

	[ii]	When pronouncing this vowel by itself, quickly move from saying ― to ㅣ. However, when paired with any consonant except for ㅇ, such as �늬 or 희, this vowel is pronounced the same as ㅣ.

ㅢ

Syllable block	Stroke order	Practice here
C / V / V	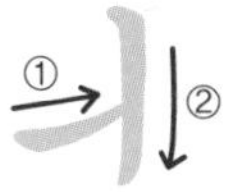 ①→ ㅢ ②↓	의 의 의 의 의 의

 **Quick Quiz**

Check to see how much you remember!

1. What does ㅝ sound like?

(1) "we" as in "western"

(2) "wa" as in "swan"

(3) "wo" as in "wonderful"

(4) "we" as in "weekend"

2. Which ㅢ sounds different from the other three?

(1) 의

(2) 희

(3) 늬

(4) 괴

3. Choose the letter which sounds different from the other three.

(1) ㅟ

(2) ㅙ

(3) ㅞ

(4) ㅚ

Listen to the audio track and circle the syllable you hear.

Q18   4. (1) 와   (2) 워   (3) 왜   (4) 위

Q19   5. (1) 와워   (2) 웨위   (3) 의위   (4) 왜워

Q20   6. (1) 놔   (2) 뭐   (3) 눼   (4) 붜

Q21   7. (1) 놔줘   (2) 눠줘   (3) 놔줴   (4) 눠줴

Answers are on p. 155.

Drills and Exercises (Unit IV ~ Unit V)

Fill in the chart

	ㅑ	ㅕ	ㅛ	ㅠ	ㅐ	ㅔ	ㅘ	ㅝ	ㅙ	ㅞ	ㅚ	ㅟ	ㅢ
ㄱ	갸												
ㄴ	냐												
ㄷ													
ㄹ													
ㅁ													
ㅂ													
ㅅ													
ㅇ													
ㅈ													

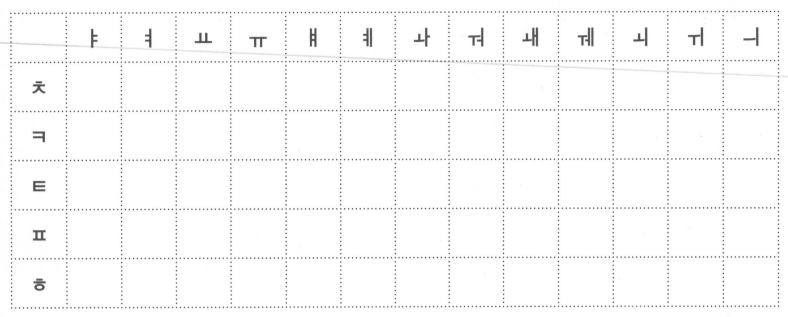

	ㅑ	ㅕ	ㅛ	ㅠ	ㅒ	ㅖ	ㅘ	ㅝ	ㅙ	ㅞ	ㅚ	ㅟ	ㅢ
ㅊ													
ㅋ													
ㅌ													
ㅍ													
ㅎ													

Answers are on p. 155.

Listen to the audio track and complete the syllable. 🎤 **Q22**

ㅈ	ㄷ	ㄱ	ㅌ			
			ㅛ	ㅖ	ㅚ	ㅑ

Answers are on p. 156.

Chapter III. Learn Hangeul

Practice reading and writing Korean words using what you have learned so far. Track 7

   귀 __ __

          __ __

시계 __ __

          __ __

뇌 __ __

          __ __

   우유 __ __

                      __ __

의사 ___ ___

___ ___

사과 ___ ___

___ ___

의자 ___ ___

___ ___

돼지 ___ ___

___ ___

가위 ___ __ __

과자 ___ __ __
                 __ __ __

The following Korean words are all loanwords. Read each loanword aloud and mark the equivalent English word.

티슈   (1) teasing   (2) t-shoes   (3) t-shirt   (4) tissue

웨이터   (1) wait   (2) way train   (3) waiter   (4) water

키위   (1) keyword   (2) kiwi   (3) keyway   (4) Key West

와이프   (1) wife   (2) whimper   (3) wipe   (4) wiper

화이트보드   (1) Hawaii too bored (2) height board (3) hardboard   (4) whiteboard

Answers are on p. 156.

Unit VI. Bat-chim (받침, Final Consonants)

Place the palm of your hand directly in front of your mouth and say the word "cat" as you would normally. There will be a slight puff of air that hits your hand when you pronounce the "t". Now say the word "cat" again, but do not let any air hit your hand when you say the "t". Remember what this feels like, as this is the general feeling you want when you say any of these Hangeul letters as a 받침.

Hangeul	IPA	Sounds like
ㄱ	[g̚] [k̚]	As a 받침, ㄱ and ㅋ do not make any sound. Take the word "doctor" and say it as two syllables, "doc" and "tor". When saying "doc", the air and the sound is completely stopped by the throat tightening up and the back of the tongue rising to block the sound and air. This is the feeling you want when ㄱ or ㅋ is a 받침.

	Syllable block	Stroke order	Practice here
ㄱ	C V / C / C V C	ㄱ①	악 악 악 옥 옥 옥

Hangeul	IPA	Sounds like
ㅋ	[k̚] [kʰ̚]	see ㄱ

	Syllable block	Stroke order	Practice here
ㅋ	C V / C / C V C	ㅋ① →②↓	엌 엌 엌 읔 읔 읔

Hangeul	IPA	Sounds like
	[n˺]	"n" as in "can" or "again"

ㄴ

Syllable block	Stroke order	Practice here
C V / C — C V C		안 안 안 온 온 온

	IPA	Sounds like
	[d˺] [t˺]	"t" as in "cat" or "bat" When it is used as **받침**, there is no puff of air after the "t" like there is in English.

ㄷ

Syllable block	Stroke order	Practice here
C V / C — C V C		얻 얻 얻 곧 곧 곧

	IPA	Sounds like
	[s˺] [ɕ˺]	see ㄷ

ㅅ

Syllable block	Stroke order	Practice here
C V / C — C V C		앗 앗 앗 옷 옷 옷

Hangeul	IPA	Sounds like
	[dʑˀ] [tɕˀ]	see ㄷ

ㅈ

Syllable block	Stroke order	Practice here
C V / C / C V C		엊 엊 엊 곳 곳 곳

	[tɕʰˀ]	see ㄷ

ㅊ

Syllable block	Stroke order	Practice here
C V / C / C V C		갖 갖 갖 옻 옻 옻

	[tˀ] [tʰˀ]	see ㄷ

ㅌ

Syllable block	Stroke order	Practice here
C V / C / C V C		앝 앝 앝 읕 읕 읕

ㅎ

[h̚]

see ㄷ

Syllable block	Stroke order	Practice here

양 양 양 응 응 응

ㄹ

[r̚]
[l̚]

This sounds similar to "l" in English when it is used as 받침, but the tip of the tongue should touch the roof of the mouth rather than sit between the teeth as it does with an English "l".

알 알 알 올 올 올

ㅁ

[m̚]

"m" as in "beam" or "team"

암 암 암 옴 옴 옴

Hangeul	IPA	Sounds like
	[b̚]	"p" as in "cap" or "tap"
	[p̚]	

ㅂ

Syllable block	Stroke order	Practice here
C V / C ‖ C V C C		압 압 압 옵 옵 옵

	[p̚]	see ㅂ
	[pʰ̚]	

ㅍ

Syllable block	Stroke order	Practice here
C V / C ‖ C V C C		앞 앞 앞 읖 읖 읖

	[ŋ̚]	"ng" as in "ring" or "song" only when used as 받침

ㅇ

Syllable block	Stroke order	Practice here
C V / C ‖ C V C C		앙 앙 앙 옹 옹 옹

 **Quick Quiz**

Check your understanding of 받침 with this quiz!

1. Choose the letter which sounds different from the other three when it is used as 받침(Bat-chim).

    (1) ㄱ

    (2) ㄷ

    (3) ㅅ

    (4) ㅈ

2. Which consonant sounds the same as ㅂ when it is used as 받침(Bat-chim)?

    (1) ㅁ

    (2) ㅊ

    (3) ㅍ

    (4) ㅎ

3. What does ㅇ sound like when it is used as 받침(Bat-chim)?

    (1) It does not make any sound.

    (2) It sounds like "h" as in "harmony" or "hat".

    (3) It sounds the same as ㄷ.

    (4) It sounds like "ng" as in "song" or "ring".

4. If this consonant is placed in front of a vowel, it is pronounced differently than if it is in the 받침 (final position). Which consonant does this best describe?

    (1) ㅁ

    (2) ㄴ

    (3) ㅍ

    (4) ㅊ

Listen to the audio track and circle the syllable you hear.

Q23 : 5. (1) 감 (2) 간 (3) 갈 (4) 갑

Q24 : 6. (1) 솜 (2) 송 (3) 손 (4) 솔

Q25 : 7. (1) 손님 (2) 솔림 (3) 송임 (4) 소님

Answers are on p. 156.

Unit VII. Double Consonants (쌍자음)

Hangeul	IPA	Sounds like
	[k']	"ch" after "s" in English, such as in the word "school" or "scheme"

ㄲ

Syllable block		Stroke order	Practice here
C V	C / V		까 까 까 꼬 꼬 꼬

| | [t'] | "t" after "s" in English, such as in the word "stress" or "steal" |

ㄸ

Syllable block		Stroke order	Practice here
C V	C / V		따 따 따 또 또 또

Hangeul	IPA	Sounds like

[p']

"p" after "s" in English, such as in the word "speech" or "spoon"

Syllable block	Stroke order	Practice here

빠 빠 빠 뽀 뽀 뽀

[s']

"s" as in "sit" or "subway"

싸 싸 싸 쏘 쏘 쏘

[c']

Make this sound by tightening the throat while pronouncing ㅈ. There is no exact equivalent sound in English, but a similar sound would be a tensed "j" as in "judge" or "jug".

짜 짜 짜 쪼 쪼 쪼

 *Quick Quiz*

Take this quiz to see how much you remember!

 Listen to the audio track and circle the syllable you hear.

1. Five of the fourteen consonants are doubled to form the five tense (fortis) consonants. Which consonant cannot be doubled to form 쌍자음?

    (1) ㄱ

    (2) ㄴ

    (3) ㄷ

    (4) ㅈ

2. What does ㅃ sound like?

    (1) "t" as in "stress"

    (2) "ch" as in "school"

    (3) "p" as in "speech"

    (4) "s" as in "sit"

🎤 **Q26**   3. (1) 방   (2) 빵   (3) 팡

🎤 **Q27**   4. (1) 금   (2) 끔   (3) 큼

🎤 **Q28**   5. (1) 땀   (2) 담   (3) 탐

🎤 **Q29**   6. (1) 장   (2) 짱   (3) 창

🎤 **Q30**   7. (1) 선   (2) 썬   (3) 전

Answers are on p. 156.

Unit VIII. Compound Consonants as Bat-chim (겹받침)

Although there are 5 types of double consonants (ㄲ, ㄸ, ㅃ, ㅆ, ㅉ), only ㄲ and ㅆ can be used as bat-chim (받침).

There are 11 "compound consonants" that look like double consonants, but are used only as bat-chims (final consonants). With these compound consonants, they take on the sound of the first consonant unless otherwise noted.

Hangeul	Sounds like
	ㄱ only - When followed by a vowel, ㅅ is pronounced with the vowel. 넋을 = [넉슬 → 넉쓸]
	ㄴ only - When followed by a vowel, ㅈ is pronounced with the vowel. 앉아 = [안자]
	ㄴ only - ㅎ is only pronounced when it is followed by ㄱ, ㄷ, or ㅈ, which are then changed to their more aspirated versions, ㅋ, ㅌ, or ㅊ. 않고 = [안코] 않다 = [안타] 않지 = [안치]

Hangeul	Sounds like

- When followed by a vowel, ㄱ is pronounced with the vowel.

읽을 = [일글]

- When not followed by a vowel, the sound is ㄱ.

읽다 = [익다 → 익따]　　　　　**읽는** = [익는 → 잉는]

- Exceptions: **읽고** = [일고 → 일꼬]

- When followed by a vowel, ㅁ is pronounced with the vowel.

젊은 = [절믄]

- When not followed by a vowel, the sound is ㅁ.

젊다 = [점다 → 점따]

ㄹ only
- When followed by a vowel, ㅂ is pronounced with the vowel.

밟아 = [발바]

- Exceptions: **밟다** = [밥다 → 밥따]

ㄹ only
- When followed by a vowel, ㅌ is pronounced with the vowel.

핥아 = [할타]

Hangeul	Sounds like

ㄹ only

- When followed by a vowel, ㅅ is pronounced with the vowel.

곬이 = [골시 → 골씨]

- There are not many words in modern Korean that have this final consonant.

- When followed by a vowel, ㅍ is pronounced with the vowel.

읊어 = [을퍼]

- When followed by a consonant, ㅍ is changed to ㅂ and becomes the representative sound.

읊다 = [읍다 → 읍따]

ㄹ only

- ㅎ is only pronounced when it is followed by ㄱ, ㄷ, or ㅈ, which are then changed to their more aspirated versions, ㅋ, ㅌ, or ㅊ.

앓고 = [알코] 앓다 = [알타] 앓지 = [알치]

ㅂ only

- When followed by a vowel, ㅅ is pronounced with the vowel.

없어 = [업서 → 업써]

 **Quick Quiz**

Check to see how much you remember!

1. Which of the following is the correct pronunciation for 않아요?

(1) [아하요]

(2) [안차요]

(3) [아나요]

(4) [안타요]

2. Which of the following is the correct pronunciation of 닭다?

(1) [달다]

(2) [담따]

(3) [달마]

(4) [달마다]

Listen to the audio track and circle the word you hear.

Q31 3. (1) 없어요 (2) 업어요 (3) 엎어요

Q32 4. (1) 널븐 (2) 넓은 (3) 넙른

Q33 5. (1) 발므면 (2) 밟으면 (3) 바쁘면

Answers are on p. 156.

Unit IX. Linking Sounds in Korean

Track II

When pronounced fast and naturally, some consonants in Korean are linked together to form a different sound than what it appears to sound like based on how it is written. This process is called "consonant assimilation" and is also used in many other languages. Considering that most native speakers of any language speak quite fast, it may be difficult to spot and understand these assimilations. When speaking or reading Korean, however, the pronunciation rules regarding consonant assimilation are quite simple as they follow the "ease of pronunciation" principle, or changing the way a word is said.

The first and most fundamental pronunciation rule is called "re-syllabification". When a syllable ends with a final consonant and is followed by a syllable that begins with ㅇ, such as in 맞아, it looks as if it would be pronounced distinctly as two different syllables, 맞 [mat] then 아 [a], with a staccato, or separation of sound. This is too awkward and difficult when speaking quickly, therefore the ㅈ becomes part of the 아, and the resulting sound is [마자].

Here are a few more examples to help you get the hang of it:

잡을 → [자블]

꽃이 → [꼬치]

책에 → [채게]

The actual spelling of the word never changes, it is only the pronunciation that is modified.

Let's get right into the nitty-gritty!

ㅎ + ㄱ, ㄷ, or ㅈ

When ㅎ is the final consonant and is combined with ㄱ, ㄷ, or ㅈ, think of it as helping create an additional puff of air needed to say the aspirated consonants ㅋ, ㅌ, or ㅊ.

Examples:

1. 놓고 → [노코]
2. 좋다 → [조타]
3. 그렇지 → [그러치]

ㅎ + ㄴ

As a final consonant, ㅎ changes to ㄴ when the following syllable begins with ㄴ.

Example:

1. 놓는 → [논는]
2. 닿는 → [단는]

ㅎ + ㅇ

If ㅎ is the final consonant in a syllable and is followed by ㅇ, it is dropped and no sound is made. Simply move on to the next syllable.

Examples:

1. 쌓은 → [싸은]
2. 좋아 → [조아]

ㄷ + 이

When ㄷ is the final consonant of a syllable, it becomes a ㅈ sound when the following syllable is 이. The ㅇ is essentially dropped, and the ㄷ, which is now said as "ㅈ", pairs up with ㅣ and is pronounced as "지".

Examples:

1. 곧이 → [고지]
2. 굳이 → [구지]
3. 받이 → [바지]

ㅌ + 이

Similarly to ㄷ, when ㅌ is a final consonant and is followed by 이, it becomes a ㅊ sound. Again, the ㅇ is dropped and ㅊ joins forces with ㅣ so that it pronounced as "치".

Example:

1. 같이 → [가치]
2. 밭이 → [바치]

ㄷ + 히

This combination is exactly like ㅌ+이. The ㄷ, when followed by 히, transforms to a ㅊ sound. This time, the ㅎ is dropped and ㅊ is united with ㅣ so that it is pronounced as "치".

Example:

1. 닫히 → [다치]
2. 묻히 → [무치]

One of the most frequently overlooked and forgotten rules among Korean language learners is the "nasalization" rule, which is when all consonants that come before a nasal consonant (ㄴ or ㅁ) are forced to become nasal sound (ㄴ, ㅁ, or ㅇ).

ㄱ, ㅋ, or ㄲ + ㄴ

Whenever you see a letter combination of ㄱ in the final position of a syllable and it is followed by ㄴ, the ㄱ is pronounced as ㅇ.

Examples:
1. 적는 → [정는]
2. 죽는 → [중는]
3. 깎는 → [깡는]

ㄱ + ㅁ

The same principle applies to ㄱ+ㅁ as well. When ㄱ ends a syllable and the following letter is ㅁ, the ㄱ is pronounced as ㅇ.

Examples:
1. 국물 → [궁물]
2. 국민 → [궁민]

ㄷ, ㅌ, ㅅ, ㅆ, ㅈ, ㅊ, or ㅎ + ㄴ

When any of the above consonants are followed by ㄴ, the sound changes to ㄴ.

Examples:
1. 듣는 → [든는]
2. 있는 → [인는]
3. 몇 년 → [면 년]
4. 솟는 → [손는]

ㅂ, ㅍ + ㄴ or ㅂ, ㅍ + ㅁ

When ㅂ or ㅍ is followed by ㄴ or ㅁ, the ㅂ or ㅍ changes to an ㅁ sound.

Examples:
1. 업는 → [엄는]
2. 접는 → [점는]
3. 밥 먹다 → [밤 먹다]
4. 감사합니다 → [감사함니다]
5. 앞문 → [암문]

ㄴ + ㄹ

When ㄴ and ㄹ meet, the ㄴ sound is replaced by the ㄹ sound.

Check out some examples:

1. 난로 → [날로]
2. 신라 → [실라]
3. 설날 → [설랄]
4. 한라산 → [할라산]

ㅇ + ㄹ or ㅁ + ㄹ

This combination results in the ㄹ sound being replaced by an ㄴ sound.

Examples:

1. 종로 → [종노]
2. 공로 → [공노]
3. 함락 → [함낙]

These rules may seem difficult to memorize at first, but once you start applying them to your spoken language, the sounds will come together very naturally and your pronunciation will be impeccable!

Congratulations!

You are well on your way to becoming a 한글 마스터!

Drills and Exercises (Unit VI ~ Unit IX)

Combine the three letters, as in the example, to create a syllable.

Ex) ㄱ + ㅏ + ㅇ = 강　　　　　　　　ㅎ + ㅑ + ㅇ =

ㅁ + ㅗ + ㅅ =　　　　　　　　　　ㄲ + ㅡ + ㅌ =

ㄷ + ㅏ + ㅂ =　　　　　　　　　　ㄸ + ㅏ + ㅇ =

ㅂ + ㅕ + ㄱ =　　　　　　　　　　ㄱ + ㅠ + ㄹ =

ㅂ + ㅣ + ㅈ =　　　　　　　　　　ㄱ + ㅘ + ㅇ =

ㅅ + ㅜ + ㄹ =　　　　　　　　　　ㄲ + ㅝ + ㅇ =

ㅊ + ㅓ + ㄴ =　　　　　　　　　　ㅇ + ㅖ + ㅂ =

ㅎ + ㅐ + ㅁ =　　　　　　　　　　ㅇ + ㅔ + ㅅ =

Answers are on p. 156.

Listen to the audio track and complete the syllable. 🎤 **Q34**

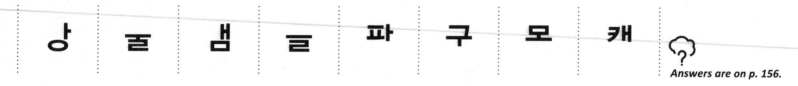

ㅏ ㄹ ㅐ ㄹ 파 구 모 캐 ☁️❓

Answers are on p. 156.

Read the following names of major cities or islands in Korea aloud, then practice writing them in Hangeul.

🎤 Track 12

서울
인천
대전
대구
대구
울산
광주
부산
제주도

인천 　　　　　　 서울 　　　　　

대전 　　　　　　 대구 　　　　　

광주 　　　　　　 울산 　　　　　

부산 　　　　　　 제주도

Look at the pictures below. Each picture is of a Korean food that is easily found in Korea. Practice reading the names of the food silently and aloud.

김밥

비빔밥

김치 부침개

된장찌개

불고기

칼국수

삼계탕

라면

삼겹살

짜장면

떡볶이

닭갈비

The following Korean words are all loanwords. Read each loanword aloud and mark the equivalent English word.

컴퓨터
(1) competition　　(2) curfew　　(3) competitor　　(4) computer

아이스크림
(1) eye cream　　(2) ice cream　　(3) eyesight　　(4) ice skater

햄버거
(1) Hamburg　　(2) Hamberg　　(3) hamburger　　(4) hand booger

메이크업
(1) makeover　　(2) Mike is up.　　(3) I will make you up.　　(4) makeup

이메일
(1) eBay　　(2) image　　(3) male　　(4) email

Answers are on p. 156.

Final Test

1. Which of the following vowels is only written to the right of consonant and can never be written below?

(1) ㅗ

(2) ㅜ

(3) ㅣ

(4) ━

2. Which of the following consonants does not make a sound when written before a vowel?

(1) ㅎ

(2) ㅇ

(3) ㅁ

(4) Both ㅎ and ㅁ

3. Which consonant sounds the same as ㄷ when it is used as 받침(Bat-chim)?

(1) ㅎ

(2) ㅁ

(3) ㄹ

(4) ㄴ

4. If you combine ㅇ, ㅛ, and ㅇ to create a syllable, which of the following is the proper way to write it?

(1) ㅇㅇ
　ㅛ

(2) ㅇㅛㅇ

(3) ㅛ
　ㅇㅇ

(4) ㅇ
　ㅛ
　ㅇ

5. Which vowel sounds like "wa" in the English word "swan"?

(1) 웨

(2) 위

(3) 와

(4) 의

6. Which of the following statements is incorrect?

(1) ㄱ and ㅋ are pronounced the same when they are used as 받침.

(2) To say ㅚ, you need to quickly move from saying ㅗ to ㅣ.

(3) ㅈ and ㅊ are pronounced the same when they are used as 받침

(4) ㅐ and ㅔ sounds almost the same, so you cannot make a distinction just by hearing them.

7. Which two of the following two words sound almost the same?

(1) 외계

(2) 위계

(3) 왜걔

(4) 웨게

8. Hangeul was promulgated by the fourth king of the Joseon Dynasty. What is the name of the king?

(1) Sejong the Great

(2) Jejong the Great

(3) Mejong the Great

(4) Rejong the Great

Listen to the audio track and circle the sound you hear.

Q35 9. 우에 / 웨

Q36 10. 우이 / 위

Q37 11. 오아 / 와

Q38 12. 우어 / 워

Q39 13. 으이 / 의

Q40 14. 우웨 / 우에

Q41 15. 오유 / 우유

Q42 16. 왜어 / 애어

Q43 17. 오아 / 오와

Q44 18. 여우 / 여으

19. Each of the following consonants change to another consonant (aspirated consonant) if you exhale more air. Which consonant do they become?.

ㄱ -> (   )

ㅈ -> (   )

ㄷ -> (   )

ㅂ -> (   )

20. Five of the fourteen consonants are doubled to form the five tense (fortis) consonants. What are they?

(   )

21. The following Korean words are loanwords that you have learned in this book. Fill in the blanks with their English translations.

아이스크림 =

햄버거 =

피자 =

버스 =

커피 =

 Dictation

22. The Korean vowel ㅗ sounds similar to "o" in English, but they are slightly different. How are the two letters different?

23. Write the answers in Hangeul according to the romanizations.

[gong] =

[pyo] =

[so-ra] =

[ji-min] =

[gim-bap] =

Q45 24. (   )

Q46 25. (   )

Q47 26. (   )

Q48 27. (   )

Q49 28. (   )

Q50 29. (   )

Q51 30. (   )

Answers are on p. 157.

Time-out #2
You Know More Korean Than You Think

Learning Korean may seem like a pretty daunting task, especially with the memorization of hundreds of new vocabulary words and all the basic grammar rules that may be completely different than the language(s) you already know. Every cloud has a silver lining, though, so do not get discouraged. The good news about learning Korean is that you already know a ton of Korean vocabulary words! Many contemporary Korean words are actually "loanwords", or words that have been borrowed from another language and are just written in Hangeul and pronounced using a Korean accent. Words dealing with technology, modern inventions, certain sports, or foods have been imported without any Chinese language influence.

If you find that you do not know the Korean word for something, or you know it and you just cannot think of it, try saying or writing the English word with a Korean pronunciation or spelling. This will not work for every English word, but someone might know what you are talking about. We do not advocate this method, as learning loanwords first before using them is best, but it does sometimes work in a pinch.

Here are some of the most common loanwords in Korean. There is no native Korean word for most of these words, so they are very similar to the original English word.

1. **콜라** = coke (can be used to refer to most big name brown-colored sodas/fizzy drinks)

2. **버스** = bus

3. **택시** = taxi

4. **텔레비전** = television

5. **테니스** = tennis

6. **컴퓨터** = computer

7. **스케이트 보드** = skateboard

There are a couple things to remember when you encounter or try to guess loanwords in Korean:

1) There are certain sounds in English that Korean does not have:
- "v" and "f" sounds are often replaced by a ㅂ, ㅃ, or ㅍ sound in Korean.

- "r" and "l" sounds are written using one Korean character, ㄹ, because the individual "r" and "l" sounds do not exist in Korean.

2) As you may have read in "Introduction to Hangeul", consonants cannot be left out on their own and must be paired with a vowel. Some English words that end with a consonant, subsequently, are paired with a vowel in Korean. It might seem a bit awkward to pronounce "bus" as 버스 at first, but rules are rules!

Flip through the pages of a Korean dictionary or look up some English words in an online Korean dictionary (not Google Translate!), you might be surprised with how many words you already know!

Chapter IV

HANGEUL HANDWRITING

Unit I. Korean Handwriting Tips

There may not be a standard or official handwriting system (aside from stroke order) that determines how Korean letters and words are to be written, but there are quite a few common traits among those who frequently write in Korean. Most of these patterns are a direct result of joining letters in a flowing manner, known as "cursive". Korean cursive is quite different from English cursive since there is no formal way to write it and it is more of a personal handwriting style. Since Korean handwriting, as with all handwriting, varies from person to person, understanding the basic idea of how certain letters can be stylized will help you better understand Korean handwriting or fancy typeface.

Each tip has three different examples, written by three different people to help you learn to identify a variety of handwriting styles and develop your own Korean handwriting.

(1) ㅏ

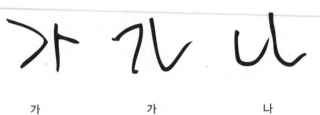

가   가   나

ㅏ often becomes ∨ or ∪ , omitting the lower half of the vertical line.

(2) ㅓ

서   어   뭐

ㅓ often becomes ㄱ , omitting the upper half of the vertical line.

(3) ㅗ

고   고   노

In a hurry to draw the horizontal line from left to right after drawing the short vertical line, many people draw the vertical and horizontal lines used to make ㅗ with one stroke, which results in a curved line and/or the omission of the left half of the horizontal line.

(4) ㅜ

누   부   부

ㅜ is often written as ㄱ , which looks nearly identical to the consonant ㄱ. The right half of the horizontal line is often omitted to save on time and limit the number of times one has to lift a writing utensil.

(5) ㄷ

ㄷ   ㄷ   도

The upper and lower horizontal lines of ㄷ are the same length in printed text, but in handwriting, the upper horizontal line tends to be longer and extend out to the left past the vertical line. This means that ㄷ can sometimes look like this: ㄹ .

(6) ㄹ

루   루   로

ㄹ is written with very sharp corners in printed text, but most people write ㄹ very curvy, almost like a backwards "s".

(7) ㅁ

마   모   무

ㅁ is rarely written like a perfect rectangle or square. The left vertical line can be very straight, but the other three sides are typically written with one stroke and are curvy and smooth. As long as it is distinguishable from ㅇ, ㅂ, or ㅍ, there is no possible confusion; therefore, depending on the person writing, ㅁ can sometimes look like a triangle or the number 12.

(8) ㅂ

바   보   부

ㅂ can be written with four straight lines, but the pen has to be lifted three times in order to do that. To lessen the amount of lifts, energy, and time it takes to write ㅂ, many people will connect lines to create two pen strokes instead of four.

(9) ㅅ

사	소	수

ㅅ is fairly easy to figure out, but sometimes the two lines can meet at the very top (apex), making it look like an upside down "v", especially when typed. When written, more often than not, the second line meets the first line in the middle. Depending on the vowel that follows, ㅅ can also appear "flattened".

(10) ㅇ

오	아	위

ㅇ is sometimes written bigger than the vowel to make it look cuter, or it can be connected to the following vowel.

(11) 오

오	오	오

오 is a combination of two very simple characters, but since it is used frequently, people tend to write it with maximum efficiency by omitting the left half of the horizontal line of ㅗ and connecting the ㅇ and ㅗ in one stroke.

(12) ㅘ

와	화	과

ㅘ is a combination of ㅗ and ㅏ, both of which can be simplified by omitting half of the longer line. ㅘ can often end up looking like ㄴ + ㄴ with ㅏ being written slightly higher than ㅗ.

해 해 행

In print, the two vertical lines of ㅐ are of the same length, but when handwritten, the first line drawn is very short, while the second line is rarely shorter than the first.

(14) 우

우 우 우

Sometimes a separation between ㅇ and ㅜ is clear in handwritten Korean; sometimes it is written with just one stroke. It is also common to see a "tail" as part of ㅇ (as seen in the middle example) which usually indicates a small lift of the pen.

(15)

의 의 의

Similarly to 우, 의 can be written using just one stroke. In order to do this, the consonant always has to be written counterclockwise. When written in one stroke, 의 can look like 외, but the line that links ㅇ and ㅢ usually ends up on the far left to avoid confusion.

(16) ㅈ

자 주 자

ㅈ is rarely ever written like it is printed. Instead of the diagonal lines (which are essentially ㅅ) touching the horizontal line in the middle, ㅈ is often written as a titled ㄱ with an additional line to the right. When written with entirely one stroke, ㅈ may sometimes look like an English "z".

(17) ᄎ

차　　　　차　　　　추

ㅊ is written similarly to ㅈ, except that the additional vertical line on the top can be attached or detached in various ways.

(18) ㅋ

카　　　　카　　　　쿠

ㅋ is pretty easy to identify, but it can sometimes be written in a way that makes it look like 구, which makes 키 look like 귀, depending on how tall or short it is written, how it is connected to the vowel, and/ or the length of the middle vertical line.

(19) ㅌ

 타　　　　투　　　　토

타　　　　투　　　　토

ㅌ is easy to understand most of the time, but you may find it written in a way that makes it look like there is a floating horizontal line over ㄷ.

(20) ㅍ

파　　　　포　　　　푸

파　　　　포　　　　푸

ㅍ has four lines in it, but depending on how many strokes it is written with, the shape can change quite a bit. Some like to link the righthand vertical line and the lower horizontal line together, making it look like ㄴ, while others may make the bottom part of ㅍ narrower than the top.

(21) ㅎ

하	호	후

The shape of ㅎ can change depending on how the two additional lines above ㅇ are connected, but the circular shape is perfectly identifiable except when ㅇ is linked with a vowel, such as in the second example.

(22) 방

방	방	방

If the characters are separated, it is easier to distinguish them, but ㅂ and ㅏ can be linked together with a line extending from ㅂ. ㅏ can also be connected to ㅇ by replacing most of the lower half of the vertical line with ㅇ.

(23) 람

람	람	람

The printed syllable 람 is quite square and angular. When handwritten, ㄹ and ㅏ are often connected and may be written without picking up the pen. ㅁ can be written as one big curvy line or in a way that makes it look like ㅣ + ㄱ with a tail.

(24) 난

난	난	난

난 often looks as if there are three of the letter ㄴ rather than two because the bottom half of ㅏ can be omitted, shortened, or connected directly to the following ㄴ.

(25) 콜라

콜라   콜라   콜라

콜라   콜라   콜라

Depending on how ㄹ is written, **콜라** can either be easy or difficult to read. Many people have a tendency to write a certain consonant or vowel in one way, and in each of the above examples, ㄹ is written twice in the same fashion.

(26) 피아노

피아노   피아노   피아노

피아노   피아노   피아노

The first and second examples are easier to read, but in the third example, ㅍ is titled to the side and connected to ㅣ. **아**, ㄴ, and ㅗ are also connected more so in the third example than the previous two.

(27) 호루라기

호루라기   호루라기   호루라기

호루라기   호루라기   호루라기

호 is often written in a fluid motion, which may make it look like an English "e" with some scribbles above. **라** and **기** are sometimes connected because the horizontal line of ㅏ can easily be the starting horizontal line of ㄱ.

(28) 호빵

호빵   호빵   호빵

호빵   호빵   호빵

Some people write ㅃ (double ㅂ) by writing ㅂ twice, while others may write it like a wide ㅂ with an additional vertical line inside.

(29) 하

하　　　하　　　하

Since 하 is the verb stem of the most commonly used verb in Korean, 하다 (to do), 하 is seen everywhere. Depending on the consonant that follows 하, the shape of 하 can remain unchanged or it can change drastically.

(30) 뭐

뭐　　　뭐　　　뭐

Since ㅜ and ㅓ often to look like ㄱ when written, 뭐 can sometimes look like ㅁ written over ㄲ (double ㄱ).

Time-Out #3
Abbreviations in Korean Slang

There are slang expressions in every language, and Korean is no exception. These days, young people often use acronyms or texting shorthand to get their message across. LOL, BRB, OMG, SMH, and WTF are just a few English examples, and just like English, Korean has this type of abbreviated lingo as well. Since these abbreviations and acronyms do not make complete sound, they are only used in writing or texting and not when speaking.

1. ㅋㅋ or ㅋㅋㅋ

This is one of the two most common ways to show the sound of laughter. Some just one letter, ㅋ. If something is extra funny, a much longer ㅋㅋㅋㅋㅋㅋㅋㅋ might be used. You can make it as long or as short as you'd like. It can be pronounced as ㅋㅋ.

2. ㅎㅎ or ㅎㅎㅎ

Using ㅎ is the second most commonly used expression to show the sound of laughter. Just like ㅋㅋ, it can be just one ㅎ or much longer. However, unlike ㅋㅋ, ㅎㅎ is either pronounced as 하하 or not said at all.

3. ㅇㅋ

This acronym comes from the English word "OK". In longer form, it would be 오케이 or 오키.

4. ㅜㅜ or ㅠㅠ

Writing or typing the vowels ㅜ or ㅠ twice makes it look like the eyes of a person who is crying or sad.

5. ㄷㄷㄷ

Triple ㄷ is used to show fear or awe. The original expression is **덜덜덜** which is an onomatopoeia used to describe the sound of trembling. **ㅎㄷㄷ** is also used, coming from **후덜덜**, which has the same meaning as **덜덜덜**.

6. ㄱㅅ or ㄸㅋ

These acronyms are shorthand for **감사합니다** or **땡큐**. Instead of actually saying "**고마워**" to a close friend, some choose to just write **ㄸㅋ** which is short for **땡큐**, or "thank you" written in Hangeul. **ㄱㅅ** or **감사합니다**, also means "thank you."

Unit II. Practice Your Handwriting

Now that you have learned all the basics of 한글, you can start developing your Korean handwriting. In this unit, you will practice writing using the tips you learned in Chapter IV, Unit I.

On each page, there is one keyword or expression with romanization and an English translation. Below the keyword are a few different styles of handwriting provided by native Korean speakers as an example of common patterns and traits that native speakers have which are much different than printed letters.

Try your hand at writing in the same pattern and style of some native speakers, then practice writing the keyword with your own personal style.

#1

가방 = bag

[ga-bang]

For each example, carefully look at the way the word was written by a native Korean in Box 1. Trace over the word in the Box 2 to get a good feel, then try your hand at writing in the same style in boxes 3 and 4!

Now practice your own handwriting here:

↣

고구마 = sweet potato
[go-gu-ma]

#2

For each example, carefully look at the way the word was written by a native Korean in Box 1. Trace over the word in the Box 2 to get a good feel, then try your hand at writing in the same style in boxes 3 and 4!

(1) 고구마 (2) 고구마   고구마   고구마

(3)   (4)

고구마   고구마   스구마   스구마

Now practice your own handwriting here:

→

 구두 = **dress shoes**

[gu-du]

#3

For each example, carefully look at the way the word was written by a native Korean in Box 1. Trace over the word in the Box 2 to get a good feel, then try your hand at writing in the same style in boxes 3 and 4!

Now practice your own handwriting here:

➜

 도로 = road

[do-ro]

For each example, carefully look at the way the word was written by a native Korean in Box 1. Trace over the word in the Box 2 to get a good feel, then try your hand at writing in the same style in boxes 3 and 4!

Now practice your own handwriting here:

➤

 모자 = **hat**
[mo-ja]

For each example, carefully look at the way the word was written by a native Korean in Box 1. Trace over the word in the Box 2 to get a good feel, then try your hand at writing in the same style in boxes 3 and 4!

Now practice your own handwriting here:

➜

바람 = wind
[ba-ram]

For each example, carefully look at the way the word was written by a native Korean in Box 1. Trace over the word in the Box 2 to get a good feel, then try your hand at writing in the same style in boxes 3 and 4!

(1) 바람 (2) 바람   바람   바람   바람   바람

(3)   (4)

바람   바람   바람   바람   바람   바람

Now practice your own handwriting here:

↪

사과 = **apple**

#7

[sa-gwa]

For each example, carefully look at the way the word was written by a native Korean in Box 1. Trace over the word in the Box 2 to get a good feel, then try your hand at writing in the same style in boxes 3 and 4!

(1) 사과 (2) 사과   사과 사과   사과 사과

(3)   (4)

사과 사과   사과 사과   사과 사과

Now practice your own handwriting here:

→

#8 손수건 = handkerchief

[son-ssu-geon]

For each example, carefully look at the way the word was written by a native Korean in Box 1. Trace over the word in the Box 2 to get a good feel, then try your hand at writing in the same style in boxes 3 and 4!

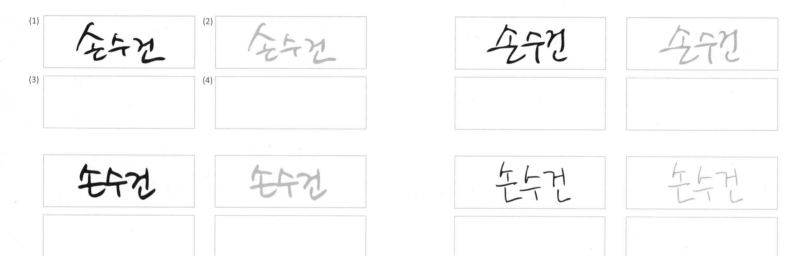

Now practice your own handwriting here:

➤

#9 스타킹 = stockings

[seu-ta-king]

For each example, carefully look at the way the word was written by a native Korean in Box 1. Trace over the word in the Box 2 to get a good feel, then try your hand at writing in the same style in boxes 3 and 4!

(1) 스타킹	(2) 스타킹	스 타 킹	스 타 킹
(3)	(4)		

스타킹	스타킹	스타킹	스타킹

Now practice your own handwriting here:

↣

신발 = shoes
[sin-bal]

For each example, carefully look at the way the word was written by a native Korean in Box 1. Trace over the word in the Box 2 to get a good feel, then try your hand at writing in the same style in boxes 3 and 4!

Now practice your own handwriting here:

↠

 아저씨 = **middle-aged man**

[a-jeo-ssi]

For each example, carefully look at the way the word was written by a native Korean in Box 1. Trace over the word in the Box 2 to get a good feel, then try your hand at writing in the same style in boxes 3 and 4!

(1) 아저씨   (2) 아저씨   아저씨   아저씨

(3)   (4)

아저씨   아저씨   아저씨   아저씨

Now practice your own handwriting here:

➟

양말 = socks

[yang-mal]

For each example, carefully look at the way the word was written by a native Korean in Box 1. Trace over the word in the Box 2 to get a good feel, then try your hand at writing in the same style in boxes 3 and 4!

(1) 양말 (2) 양말 양말 양말 양말 양말

(3)

양맏 양맏 양말 양말 양말 양말

Now practice your own handwriting here:

↦

 **오리** = duck
[o-ri]

For each example, carefully look at the way the word was written by a native Korean in Box 1. Trace over the word in the Box 2 to get a good feel, then try your hand at writing in the same style in boxes 3 and 4!

Now practice your own handwriting here:

➤

의사 = doctor
[ui-sa]

For each example, carefully look at the way the word was written by a native Korean in Box 1. Trace over the word in the Box 2 to get a good feel, then try your hand at writing in the same style in boxes 3 and 4!

Now practice your own handwriting here:

→

 **장난감** = toy

[jang-nan-kkam]

For each example, carefully look at the way the word was written by a native Korean in Box 1. Trace over the word in the Box 2 to get a good feel, then try your hand at writing in the same style in boxes 3 and 4!

(1)  | (2)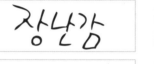
|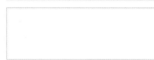

(3) | (4)

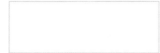 |

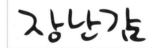 |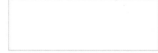

Now practice your own handwriting here:

➝

#16 **주차장** = **parking lot**
[ju-cha-jang]

For each example, carefully look at the way the word was written by a native Korean in Box 1. Trace over the word in the Box 2 to get a good feel, then try your hand at writing in the same style in boxes 3 and 4!

(1) 주차장 (2) 주차장   주차장   주차장

(3)   (4)

주차장   주차장   주차장   주차장

Now practice your own handwriting here:

➤

초콜렛 = chocolate

[cho-col-let]

For each example, carefully look at the way the word was written by a native Korean in Box 1. Trace over the word in the Box 2 to get a good feel, then try your hand at writing in the same style in boxes 3 and 4!

(1)
(2)
(3)
(4)

Now practice your own handwriting here:

➥

촛불 = candlelight

[chot-bul]

For each example, carefully look at the way the word was written by a native Korean in Box 1. Trace over the word in the Box 2 to get a good feel, then try your hand at writing in the same style in boxes 3 and 4!

(1) 촛불

(2) 촛불

촛불

촛불

촛불

촛불

(3)

(4) .

촛불

촛불

촛불

촛불

Now practice your own handwriting here:

➤

콜라 = cola

[col-la]

For each example, carefully look at the way the word was written by a native Korean in Box 1. Trace over the word in the Box 2 to get a good feel, then try your hand at writing in the same style in boxes 3 and 4!

(1) 콜라　(2) 콜라

(3)　(4)

콜라　콜라

콜라　콜라

콜라　콜라

Now practice your own handwriting here:

➤

피아노 = **piano**

[pi-a-no]

For each example, carefully look at the way the word was written by a native Korean in Box 1. Trace over the word in the Box 2 to get a good feel, then try your hand at writing in the same style in boxes 3 and 4!

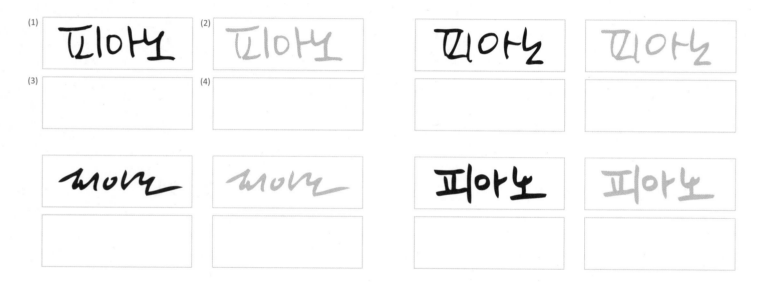

Now practice your own handwriting here:

→

호랑이 = tiger
[ho-rang-i]

For each example, carefully look at the way the word was written by a native Korean in Box 1. Trace over the word in the Box 2 to get a good feel, then try your hand at writing in the same style in boxes 3 and 4!

(1) 호랑이   (2) 호랑이   호랑이   호랑이

(3)   (4)

호랑이   호랑이   호랑이   호랑이

Now practice your own handwriting here:

➤

 **호루라기** = **whistle**
#22
[ho-ru-ra-gi]

For each example, carefully look at the way the word was written by a native Korean in Box I. Trace over the word in the Box 2 to get a good feel, then try your hand at writing in the same style in boxes 3 and 4!

(1) 호루라기　(2) 호루라기　　호루라기　호루라기

(3)　　　　　(4)

호루라기　호루라기　　호루라기　호루라기

Now practice your own handwriting here:

➜

#23 호빵 = steamed bun
[ho-ppang]

For each example, carefully look at the way the word was written by a native Korean in Box 1. Trace over the word in the Box 2 to get a good feel, then try your hand at writing in the same style in boxes 3 and 4!

(1) (2)
(3) (4)

Now practice your own handwriting here:

➼

#24 감사합니다. = **Thank you.**

[gam-sa-ham-ni-da.]

For each example, carefully look at the way the word was written by a native Korean in Box 1. Trace over the word in the Box 2 to get a good feel, then try your hand at writing in the same style in boxes 3 and 4!

(1) 감사합니다. (2) 감사합니다.

감사합니다. 감사합니다.

(3)

(4)

감사합니다. 감사합니다.

감사합니다. 감사합니다.

Now practice your own handwriting here:

➵

고맙습니다. = Thank you.

#25

[go-map-seum-ni-da.]

For each example, carefully look at the way the word was written by a native Korean in Box 1. Trace over the word in the Box 2 to get a good feel, then try your hand at writing in the same style in boxes 3 and 4!

(1) 고맙습니다.

(2) 고맙습니다.

고맙습니다.

고맙습니다.

(3)

(4)

고맙습니다.

고맙습니다.

고맙습니다.

고맙습니다.

Now practice your own handwriting here:

➙

#26 괜찮아요. = I'm okay.

[gwaen-cha-na-yo.]

For each example, carefully look at the way the word was written by a native Korean in Box 1. Trace over the word in the Box 2 to get a good feel, then try your hand at writing in the same style in boxes 3 and 4!

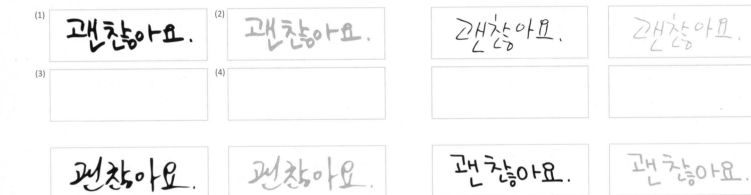

(1) 괜찮아요.   (2) 괜찮아요.   괜찮아요.   괜찮아요

(3)   (4)

괜찮아요.   괜찮아요.   괜찮아요.   괜찮아요

Now practice your own handwriting here:

➜

너무 예뻐요. = It's so pretty.

[neo-mu ye-ppeo-yo.]

For each example, carefully look at the way the words were written by a native Korean in Box 1. Trace over the words in the Box 2 to get a good feel, then try your hand at writing in the same style in boxes 3 and 4!

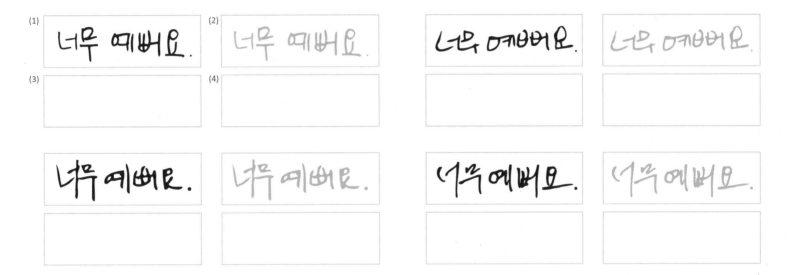

Now practice your own handwriting here:

➤

#28

다음에 또 만나요. = See you again.

[da-eu-me tto man-na-yo.]

For each example, carefully look at the way the words were written by a native Korean in Box 1. Trace over the words in the Box 2 to get a good feel, then try your hand at writing in the same style in boxes 3 and 4!

(1)

다음에 또 만나요.　　다음에 또 만나요.　　다음에 또 만나요.

(2)

다음에 또 만나요.　　다음에 또 만나요.　　다음에 또 만나요.

(3)

(4)

Now practice your own handwriting here:

➤

29

도와줘서 고마워요. = **Thank you for helping me.**

[do-wa-jwo-seo go-ma-wo-yo.]

For each example, carefully look at the way the words were written by a native Korean in Box 1. Trace over the words in the Box 2 to get a good feel, then try your hand at writing in the same style in boxes 3 and 4!

(1)

| 도와줘서 고마워요. | 도와줘서 고마워요. | 도와줘서 고마워요. |

(2)

| 도와줘서 고마워요. | 도와줘서 고마워요. | 도와줘서 고마워요. |

(3)

(4)

Now practice your own handwriting here:

➜

마음에 들었으면 좋겠어요. = I hope you like it.

[ma-eu-me deu-reo-sseu-myeon jo-ke-sseo-yo.]

For each example, carefully look at the way the words were written by a native Korean in Box 1. Trace over the words in the Box 2 to get a good feel, then try your hand at writing in the same style in boxes 3 and 4!

(1)

마음에 들었으면 좋겠어요.

마음에 들었으면 좋겠어요.

마음에 들었으면 좋겠어요.

(2)

마음에 들었으면 좋겠어요.

마음에 들었으면 좋겠어요.

마음에 들었으면 좋겠어요.

(3)

(4)

Now practice your own handwriting here:

➥

#31 # 만나서 반가웠어요. = **Nice meeting you.**

[man-na-seo ban-ga-wo-sseo-yo.]

For each example, carefully look at the way the words were written by a native Korean in Box 1. Trace over the words in the Box 2 to get a good feel, then try your hand at writing in the same style in boxes 3 and 4!

(1)

| 만나서 반가웠어요. | 만나서 반가웠어요. | 만나서 반가웠어요. |

(2)

| 만나서 반가웠어요. | 만나서 반가웠어요. | 만나서 반가웠어요. |

(3)

(4)

Now practice your own handwriting here:

➜

#32 맛있게 드세요. = Enjoy your meal.

[ma-sit-ge deu-se-yo.]

For each example, carefully look at the way the words were written by a native Korean in Box 1. Trace over the words in the Box 2 to get a good feel, then try your hand at writing in the same style in boxes 3 and 4!

(1) 맛있게 드세요.

(2) 맛있게 드세요.

맛있게 드세요.

맛있게 드세요.

(3)

(4)

맛있게 드세요.

맛있게 드세요.

맛있게 드세요.

맛있게 드세요.

Now practice your own handwriting here:

➔

메리 크리스마스.
[me-ri keu-ri-seu-ma-seu.]

= Merry Christmas.

#33

For each example, carefully look at the way the words were written by a native Korean in Box 1. Trace over the words in the Box 2 to get a good feel, then try your hand at writing in the same style in boxes 3 and 4!

(1)

메리 크리스마스.　　　메러 크리스마스.　　　네리 크리스마스.

(2)

메리 크리스마스.　　　메러 크리스마스.　　　네리 크리스마스.

(3)

(4)

Now practice your own handwriting here:

➤

새해 복 많이 받으세요. = **Happy New Year.**

[sae-hae bok ma-ni ba-deu-se-yo.]

For each example, carefully look at the way the words were written by a native Korean in Box 1. Trace over the words in the Box 2 to get a good feel, then try your hand at writing in the same style in boxes 3 and 4!

(1)

| 새해 복 많이 받으세요. | 새해 복 많이 받으세요. | 새해 복 많이 받으세요. |

(2)

| 새해 복 많이 받으세요. | 새해 복 많이 받으세요. | 새해 복 많이 받으세요. |

(3)

(4)

Now practice your own handwriting here:

#35 ## 생일 축하해요. = **Happy Birthday.**

[saeng-il chu-ka-hae-yo.]

For each example, carefully look at the way the words were written by a native Korean in Box 1. Trace over the words in the Box 2 to get a good feel, then try your hand at writing in the same style in boxes 3 and 4!

(1) 생일 축하해요.

(2) 생일 축하해요.

생일 축하해요.

생일 축하해요.

(3)

(4)

생일 축하해요.

생일 축하해요.

생일 축하해요.

생일 축하해요.

Now practice your own handwriting here:

#36

식사 맛있게 하세요.

[sik-sa ma-sit-ge ha-se-yo.]

= **Enjoy your meal.**

For each example, carefully look at the way the words were written by a native Korean in Box 1. Trace over the words in the Box 2 to get a good feel, then try your hand at writing in the same style in boxes 3 and 4!

(1)

| 식사 맛있게 하세요. | 식사 맛있게 하세요. | 식사 맛있게 하세요. |

(2)

| 식사 맛있게 하세요. | 식사 맛있게 하세요. | 식사 맛있게 하세요. |

(3)

(4)

Now practice your own handwriting here:

#37 안녕하세요. = **Hello.**

[an-nyeong-ha-se-yo.]

For each example, carefully look at the way the word was written by a native Korean in Box 1. Trace over the word in the Box 2 to get a good feel, then try your hand at writing in the same style in boxes 3 and 4!

(1) 안녕하세요.

(2) 안녕하세요.

안녕하세요.

안녕하세요.

(3)

(4)

안녕하세요.

안녕하세요.

안녕하세요.

안녕하세요.

Now practice your own handwriting here:

↣

#38

안녕히 가세요. = (to someone leaving) Good-bye.

[an-nyeong-hi ga-se-yo.]

For each example, carefully look at the way the words were written by a native Korean in Box 1. Trace over the words in the Box 2 to get a good feel, then try your hand at writing in the same style in boxes 3 and 4!

(1) 안녕히 가세요. (2) 안녕히 가세요.

(3) (4)

안녕히 가세요. 안녕히 가세요.

안녕히 가세요. 안녕히 가세요.

안녕히 가세요. 안녕히 가세요.

Now practice your own handwriting here:

→

#39

안녕히 계세요.
= (to someone staying) Good-bye.

[an-nyeong-hi gye-se-yo.]

For each example, carefully look at the way the words were written by a native Korean in Box 1. Trace over the words in the Box 2 to get a good feel, then try your hand at writing in the same style in boxes 3 and 4!

(1) 안녕히 계세요.

(2) 안녕히 계세요.

안녕히 계세요.

안녕히 계세요.

(3)

(4)

안녕히 계세요.

안녕히 계세요.

안녕히 계세요.

안녕히 계세요.

Now practice your own handwriting here:

➤

#40 여기는 어떻게 가요? = How do you get there?

[yeo-gi-neun eo-tteo-ke ga-yo?]

For each example, carefully look at the way the words were written by a native Korean in Box 1. Trace over the words in the Box 2 to get a good feel, then try your hand at writing in the same style in boxes 3 and 4!

(1)	여기는 어떻게 가요?	여기는 어떻게 가요?	여기는 어떻게 가요?
(2)	여기는 어떻게 가요?	여기는 어떻게 가요?	여기는 어떻게 가요?
(3)			
(4)			

Now practice your own handwriting here:

→

오늘 뭐 할 거예요? = **What will you do today?**

[o-neul mwo hal geo-ye-yo?]

For each example, carefully look at the way the words were written by a native Korean in Box 1. Trace over the words in the Box 2 to get a good feel, then try your hand at writing in the same style in boxes 3 and 4!

(1)

| 오늘 뭐 할 거예요? | 오늘 뭐 할 거예요? | 오늘 뭐 할 거예요? |

(2)

| 오늘 뭐 할 거예요? | 오늘 뭐 할 거예요? | 오늘 뭐 할 거예요? |

(3)

(4)

Now practice your own handwriting here:

➜

#42

월화수목금토일 = Monday through Sunday

[wo-rwa-su-mok-geum-to-il]

For each example, carefully look at the way the words were written by a native Korean in Box 1. Trace over the words in the Box 2 to get a good feel, then try your hand at writing in the same style in boxes 3 and 4!

(1)	월화수목금토일	월화수목금토일	월화수목금토일
(2)	월화수목금토일	월화수목금토일	월화수목금토일
(3)			
(4)			

Now practice your own handwriting here:

→

이거 뭐예요? = What is this?

[i-geo mwo-ye-yo?]

For each example, carefully look at the way the words were written by a native Korean in Box 1. Trace over the words in the Box 2 to get a good feel, then try your hand at writing in the same style in boxes 3 and 4!

(1) **이거 뭐예요?**

(2) 이거 뭐예요?

이거 뭐예요?

이거 뭐예요?

(3)

(4)

이거 뭐예요?

이거 뭐예요?

이거 뭐예요?

이거 뭐예요?

Now practice your own handwriting here:

➜

이따가 전화해 주세요. = Call me later.

[i-tta-ga jeo-nwa-hae ju-se-yo.]

For each example, carefully look at the way the words were written by a native Korean in Box 1. Trace over the words in the Box 2 to get a good feel, then try your hand at writing in the same style in boxes 3 and 4!

(1)

| 이따가 전화해 주세요. | 이따가 전화해 주세요. | 이따가 전화해 주세요. |

(2)

| 이따가 전화해 주세요. | 이따가 전화해 주세요. | 이따가 전화해 주세요. |

(3)

(4)

Now practice your own handwriting here:

#45

잘 먹겠습니다.

= I'll eat well.

[jal meok-ge-sseum-ni-da.]

For each example, carefully look at the way the words were written by a native Korean in Box 1. Trace over the words in the Box 2 to get a good feel, then try your hand at writing in the same style in boxes 3 and 4!

(1)

| 잘 먹겠습니다. | 잘 먹겠습니다. | 잘 먹겠습니다. |

(2)

| 잘 먹겠습니다. | 잘 먹겠습니다. | 잘 먹겠습니다. |

(3)

| | | |

(4)

| | | |

Now practice your own handwriting here:

잘 먹었습니다. = I ate well.

#46

[jal meo-geo-sseum-ni-da.]

For each example, carefully look at the way the words were written by a native Korean in Box 1. Trace over the words in the Box 2 to get a good feel, then try your hand at writing in the same style in boxes 3 and 4!

(1)

| 잘 먹었습니다. | 잘 먹었습니다. | 잘 먹었습니다. |

(2)

| 잘 먹었습니다. | 잘 먹었습니다. | 잘 먹었습니다. |

(3)

(4)

Now practice your own handwriting here:

→

#47

저녁에 뭐 먹고 싶어요? = **What do you want to eat for dinner?**

[jeo-nyeo-ge mwo meok-go si-peo-yo?]

For each example, carefully look at the way the words were written by a native Korean in Box 1. Trace over the words in the Box 2 to get a good feel, then try your hand at writing in the same style in boxes 3 and 4!

(1)

| 저녁에 뭐 먹고 싶어요! | 저녁에 뭐먹고 싶어요? | 저녁에 뭐 먹고 싶어요? |

(2)

| 저녁에 뭐 먹고 싶어요! | 저녁에 뭐먹고 싶어요? | 저녁에 뭐 먹고 싶어요? |

(3)

(4)

Now practice your own handwriting here:

#48 좋은 하루 보내세요. = **Have a good day.**

[jo-eun ha-ru bo-nae-se-yo.]

For each example, carefully look at the way the words were written by a native Korean in Box 1. Trace over the words in the Box 2 to get a good feel, then try your hand at writing in the same style in boxes 3 and 4!

(1)

| 좋은 하루 보내세요. | 좋은 하루 보내세요. | 좋은 하루 보내세요. |

(2)

| 좋은 하루 보내세요. | 좋은 하루 보내세요. | 좋은 하루 보내세요. |

(3)

(4)

Now practice your own handwriting here:

퇴근하고 만나요. = Let's meet after work.

#49

[toe-geu-na-go man-na-yo.]

For each example, carefully look at the way the words were written by a native Korean in Box 1. Trace over the words in the Box 2 to get a good feel, then try your hand at writing in the same style in boxes 3 and 4!

(1)

| 퇴근 하고 만나요. | 퇴근하고 만나요. | 퇴근하고 만나요. |

(2)

| 퇴근 하고 만나요. | 퇴근하고 만나요. | 퇴근하고 만나요. |

(3)

(4)

Now practice your own handwriting here:

➟

행복하세요. = Be happy.

#50

[haeng-bo-ka-se-yo.]

For each example, carefully look at the way the word was written by a native Korean in Box 1. Trace over the word in the Box 2 to get a good feel, then try your hand at writing in the same style in boxes 3 and 4!

(1) 행복하세요.

(2) 행복하세요.

행복하세요.

행복하세요.

(3)

(4)

행복하세요.

행복하세요.

행복하세요.

행복하세요.

Now practice your own handwriting here:

➜

Time-Out #4
Shortening Sentences Without Sacrificing Meaning

With Hangeul, you can express more with fewer words than with English. Perhaps not with everything, but most of the time you can shorten the length of a sentence. This is especially useful when writing on social media or in text messages where you only have a set number of characters for your message.

Take, for example, the word "coffee". In English, it's spelled with 6 letters, but in Hangeul, the word for "coffee" is **커피**, which is only two "letters", and it only takes up two character spaces when typing or texting!

Here are a few more examples:

ice cream *(8 letters plus 1 space)* = **아이스크림** *(5 letters)*

Canada *(6 letters)* = **캐나다** *(3 letters)*

hamburger *(9 letters)* = **햄버거** *(3 letters)*

television *(10 letters)* = **텔레비전** *(4 letters)*

Hangeul allows room to omit more things in a sentence than in English. If the context is clear, you can take out the subject, the object, or even the verb! This makes it super easy to minimize the number of letters used without sacrificing the meaning.

Examples:

1. I met my friends yesterday.
   = 저는 어제 친구들을 만났어요.
   = 저 어제 친구들 만났어요.
   = 어제 친구들 만났어요.
   = 어제 친구 만났어요.

2. I am going to go home and sleep.
   = 저는 집에 가서 잠을 잘 거예요.
   = 저는 집에 가서 잘 거예요.
   = 집에 가서 잘 거예요.
   = 집에 가 잘 거예요.

Unit III. Korean Handwriting Quiz

Ready to put your reading skills to the test?

There are 60 questions in this quiz.

Read the handwritten word or phrase and circle the typed word

which best represents the handwritten example.

Answers are on p. 158.

#1

가방

(1) ㄱ빵   (2) 개랑

(3) 가방   (4) 개방

 #2

고구마

(1) 고수마   (2) 고구마

(3) 고구라   (4) 소수마

 #3

구두

(1) 3루   (2) 구루

(3) 구두   (4) ㅕ루

 #4

도로

(1) 도로   (2) 도노

(3) 조로   (4) 조노

 #5

모자

(1) 오자   (2) 모자

(3) 조자   (4) 로자

 #6

바람

(1) 배남   (2) 어맘

(3) 바람   (4) 바락

#7

손수건

(1) 손수건　　(2) 손구건

(3) 손두건　　(4) 손쉬고

#8

피아노

(1) 개아로　　(2) 개이로

(3) 피아모　　(4) 피아노

#9

의사

(1) 의사　　(2) 외사

(3) 어사　　(4) 회사

#10

콜라

(1) 돈라　　(2) 콜라

(3) 몰라　　(4) 콜나

#11

장난감

(1) 장난간　　(2) 장쏘감

(3) 장난감　　(4) 장쏘과

#12

호랑이

(1) 코랑이　　(2) 호랑이

(3) 천랑이　　(4) 천광이

#13

(1) 초방	(2) 호방
(3) 초광	(4) 호빵

#14

전화

(1) 건화	(2) 선화
(3) 전화	(4) 전좌

#15

친구

(1) 친3	(2) 권구
(3) 권3	(4) 친구

#16

신발

(1) 신발	(2) 닌발
(3) 진발	(4) 신백

#17

노래

(1) W래	(2) 노래
(3) 나래	(4) 노태

#18

질문

(1) 질문	(2) 건문
(3) 질만	(4) 건만

#19

오리

(1) 오리   (2) 요리

(3) 우리   (4) 워리

#20

긴

(1) 긴   (2) 김

(3) 길   (4) 릴

#21

문제

(1) 운제   (2) 문제

(3) 문세   (4) 군제

#22

운동

(1) 운농   (2) 운동

(3) 운옹   (4) 안동

#23

강아지

(1) 상아시   (2) 강아지

(3) 갱아지   (4) 갱이지

#24

아이스크림

(1) 아이스크림   (2) 아이그크림

(3) 아이스군림   (4) 아이스군딤

#25

시간

(1) 시포   (2) 시모

(3) 시간   (4) 시조

#26

편의점

(1) 면의점   (2) 련의점

(3) 떤의점   (4) 편의점

#27

생각

(1) 생푸   (2) 상푸

(3) 생각   (4) 상각

#28

컴퓨터

(1) 컹루러   (2) 컹류리

(3) 컴퓨터   (4) 컴퓨리

#29

거짓말

(1) 거짓말   (2) 거짓밀

(3) 개짓밀   (4) 거짓알

#30

지하철

(1) 거하철   (2) 거바철

(3) 지하철   (4) 지하척

#31

서울

(1) 서불　　(2) 서울

(3) 개울　　(4) 저울

#32

대구

(1) 머구　　(2) 머수

(3) 대수　　(4) 대구

#33

대전

(1) 머전　　(2) 대전

(3) 대건　　(4) 머건

#34

부산

(1) 부산　　(2) 부솨

(3) 부모　　(4) 우산

#35

광주

(1) 랑구　　(2) 랑주

(3) 광주　　(4) 광수

#36

제주도

(1) 제주도　　(2) 제수도

(3) 제주W　　(4) 제누도

#37

옷

(1) 왜~   (2) 웃

(3) 옷   (4) 와

#38

학고

(1) 락교   (2) 학교

(3) 학고   (4) 착교

#39

시무실

(1) M주실   (2) 시무실

(3) 시주실   (4) 사무실

#40

네리 크리스마스

(1) 에리 크리스마스   (2) 베리 크리스마스

(3) 메리 크리스마스   (4) 네리 크리스마스

#41

안녕하세요

(1) 안ㄴㅎ하세요   (2) 안녕하세요

(3) 안녕하제요   (4) 안녕하세9ㄴ

#42

저녁에 뭐 먹고 싶어요?

(1) 2벽에 뭐 먹고 식니온?   (2) 저녁에 뭐 목고 식니온?

(3) 저녁에 뭐 먹고 싶어요?   (4) 그녁에 뭐 1걱고 싶어요?

#43

이거 뭐예요?

(1) 이ㄲ 무가기요?   (2) 이거 뭐예요?

(3) 이거 무가기요?   (4) 이3 뭐예요?

#44

좋은 하루 보내세요.

(1) 폴은 과루 보네세요   (2) 좋은 과루 보내세요

(3) 롤은 하루 보네세요   (4) 좋은 하루 보내세요

#45

괜찮아요

(1) 괜랂아요   (2) 괜찮아요

(3) 괜랂아91   (4) 괜랂아외

#46

웃지 마세요

(1) 웃지 마세요   (2) 웃지 마제요

(3) 윗지 마세요   (4) 윗지 마제요

#47

시간이 너무 빨라요

(1) 시간이 너무 빨라요   (2) 시포이 너루 빨나요

(3) 시포이 너루 발나요   (4) 시간이 너루 빨나요

#48

이거 누가 만들었어요?

(1) 이거 뉘 만들었어요?   (2) 미거 누가 만들었어요?

(3) 이거 누가 만들었어요?   (4) 미거 뉘 만들었어묘?

#49

오래 기다렸어요 ?

(1) 오해 기다렸이요?   (2) 오해 기다렸어요?

(3) 오해 기다렸어요?   (4) 오래 기다렸어요?

#50

질문이 있어요

(1) 걸몬이 있어요   (2) 질문이 있어요

(3) 질몬이 있어요   (4) 질물이 있어요

#51

운동 좋아하세요?

(1) 운릉 동아하세요?   (2) 운동 좋아하세요?

(3) 운동 동아하세요?   (4) 운릉 좋아하세요?

#52

눈을 감으세요

(1) 고을 감으서1오   (2) 눈을 감으ㅅ기요

(3) 눈을 감으세요   (4) 고을 감으세요

그 책 재미있어요?

(1) 2 책 래미있어요?　　(2) 그 책 재미있어요?

(3) 2 책 자비있어요?　　(4) 그 책 재미입어요?

거짓말 하지 마세요

(1) 거짓랄 하저 하세요　　(2) 거것랄 하지 라세요

(3) 거짓말 하지 마세요　　(4) 거것랄 하저 하세요

왜 아직도 안 자요?

(1) 오H 아직W 안 자요?　　(2) 왜 아직도 안 자요?

(3) 왜 아직로 안 자요?　　(4) 왜 아걱도 안 자요?

무서운 꿈을 꿨어요

(1) 무M은 끌을 꿨어요　　(2) 무서운 꿈을 꿨어요

(3) 무러운 꿈을 꿨이요　　(4) 무서운 꿈을 꿨어와

#57

잘 생각해 보세요

(1) 잘 생각해 몬세은　　(2) 잘 생각해 보세요

(3) 잘 생각해 부세온　　(4) 잘 생각해 보세호

#58

제 문자 받았어요

(1) 제 룬자 밭알이은　　(2) 제 문자 받았어은

(3) 제 룬자 발았어요　　(4) 제 문자 받았어요

#59

냉장고를 열어 보세요

(1) 뱅장고를 열어 넌세요　(2) 냉장고를 열어 넌세요

(3) 냉장고를 열어 보세와　(4) 냉장고를 열어 보세요

#60

저는 쇼핑하는 걸 싫어해요

(1) 저른 쇼펑하른 건 신어해요　(2) 저는 쇼핑하는 걸 싫어해요

(3) 저를 쇼핑하를 걸 싫어해요　(4) 저를 쇼링하는 걸 실어해요

Time-Out #5
Chinese characters in the Korean Language

In the "History of Hangeul", it was mentioned that, before Hangeul was invented, Koreans borrowed and modified Chinese characters (called Hanja [한자]) to represent the sound of Korean words. Many important documents were written with Chinese characters, and although most Chinese characters have been replaced with Hangeul, there are still a few characters that have made a permanent home in Korean.

So, how much Hanja do native Koreans actually know? It depends on the person, but the average Korean person who received the most basic public education was taught somewhere between a few hundred to a few thousand Hanja characters. Realistically, since Hanja is not used dominantly, most people can recognize only a couple hundred characters and can write even fewer because Hangeul makes knowledge of writing Hanja almost unnecessary.

For example, the word 전진 is a word that many people will be able to instantly recognize as having a meaning based on certain Hanja characters, 전 meaning "forward" (前) and 진 meaning "progress" (進). People may not be able to write the characters, however, simply because they have never had to write them before.